G-NOETRY:
Affairs of the Heart

Poetry about Life

By

GALUMINATTI

All rights reserved. No part of this publication may be copied, duplicated, reproduced, stored in a retrieval system, or transmitted in any form or by any means – electronic, mechanical, photocopy, recording or any other – except for brief quotations in printed reviews, without the prior permission of the publisher.

Copyright © 2008 Bathwater Press Publishing
Clinton, Maryland 20735
All rights reserved
June 2008
Printed in Canada

ISBN: 978-0-9789196-3-4   0-9789196-3-7

Library of Congress Control Number (LCCN)
2008904283

To order additional copies please contact us.
Bathwater Press Publishing
www.g-natti.com
703-597-1373

First and foremost I want to thank God for allowing me to be able to breathe and capture the moments of life that seem to go so swiftly by us. I want to thank God for giving me the determination to be persistent regardless of how many obstacles are tossed in my way, regardless of how many doors are slammed in my face, regardless of how many friends and loved ones turn on me for whatever reason, regardless of how many times I get myself into trouble. God is always there. I thank you Lord.

I also want to thank my 18 year old daughter Destaynee and my sixteen year old son, DaShawn and I cannot do so without acknowledging their mother, who raised them more so than I have.

Destaynee and DaShawn, I love you and I apologize that you two were dealt the cards that you were dealt. You are two beautiful kids who have emerged. I regret that I missed those years that you were growing up while I was somewhere off in the military serving my country. If there is one thing in life that I wish I could take back, I would turn back the hands of time and spend as much time as humanly possible with you two. I love you very dearly and you are a great source of my inspiration. I may not talk to you everyday but my heart, my spirit, my mind is always occupied with the two of you in some form or another. I think of you sometimes and I cry, because I miss you more than you know, more than I can express. Just know that I love you and I am here for you and in your corner!

Poems

Hard Words 1
Every time Seems Like The First Time 4
The Fragrance of A Rose 8
You Probably Won't Remember 10
My Pecan Tan (Dime Piece) 13
Serious Biz 16
On Being Judged 19
I Apologize 21
V-Day or D-Day 24
Hoochie's World 27
I Found A Penny Today 29
No More 31
Refuse to Break Up 33
Are You Living A Lie? 35
So Into You 37
Prejudice Eyes 38
Some Moment In Time 40
Not A Day Goes By 44
You Begin Me 47
The Aftermath 50
Why Do Women Lie? 54
But I Keep On Having These Dreams 57
My Name… Is Tyrone 60
Why Am I So Sad? 62
Left The Strong 65
Oh No She Didn't 67
The Man Barack Obama 70

Sometimes, the folks you love the most can be the very ones to hurt you the worst. This was my initial response to what I viewed as lack of support. It was very negative and it really hurt me to my spirit. I pulled over to the side of the highway and wrote these words.

<u>Hard Words</u>

Pen in my hand
Words fighting for my time
Trying to release these thoughts
That fully occupy my mind

I go shopping at the store
Because I'm a balla to the core
I take my credit card and charge it
All the way to the floor

Admirers blowing up my cell
Whispering their sweet nothings
Tempting my flesh to prevail
But I'm not about corrupting

They don't understand my drive
They think I'm here just for a simple thrill
For I seek to spiritually strive
While trying to execute God's will

What's a person to do?
They think I'm out here just to get paid

Right now is definitely not the time
I'm not even trying to get laid

Like you, I been through some things
That could have crippled my very soul
Family, institution, God!
Nobody really knows

You share with folks your obstacle course
They want to know more about your loot
Don't give a hoot about showing remorse
Instead they're trying to eat your fruit

Then the very ones you love
Who you think know you so well
Become more focused on your paper
It becomes a living hell

They don't understand your fight
But they feel they have a right
To your hard earned dough
It's no longer your show

You just happened to obtain success
Then they treat you like you're under arrest
Because according to their calculations
You owe all of them some of your nest

Oh yes, they hurt me oh so bad
Made me, oh so mad
Their shallow views and hard words
Will keep me writing on a pad

Did they ever call my house
After I lost my spouse?
When fame came, they put in their bids
Didn't even call to ask about my kids

I guess you really have to learn
To cut certain people off
They can make you stubborn and stern
They can make you feel so lost

Family, I'm just trying to get out the gate
Please learn not to hate
I'm the same ole country boy
That you used to elevate

Was the first to graduate from college
I'm just trying to utilize my knowledge
I'm still motivated by hope
Just give me some time to lower that rope

Can you please, for now, do me a favor?
And quietly let this savor
Just pray for my kids
And for their next door neighbor.

There is the possibility of meeting someone and falling in love with them to where every time you make love, it really does seem like the first time. It's an overwhelming experience that oftentimes cannot be described by words.

<u>Every Time Seems Like The First Time</u>

I was staring at her
She was staring at me
We were staring at each other
With nothing but anticipation
I looked forward to the emancipation

I wanted so badly to undress her
I think she wanted me with the same fire
My desire I was not about to retire

She did not say a mumbling word
But her eyes were talking and I clearly heard
Her moans and groans from staring
Boy, was I faring!

"If he could just take me right now
I would gladly bow"
Her eyes were talking, while I was stalking

"I would love to take you right now and give
you what you need"
My emotions took heed
My eyes, she could read

She just stood there with thought
I was intrigued and I was caught
I was captured in the rapture of her mind
She had me suspended in time
You could hear the drop of a dime

I noticed her bright and shining wedding band
She saw mine as well on my hand
Nevertheless, who between us would fall?
Who would stand?

Blue jean mini skirt, no stockings but sandals
Was my life about to become a scandal?
So I thought
White baby phat top with a rack about to drop
It like it was hot

I wore a dark green wife beater
Tan shorts, black shoes
Who was about to win?
Who was about to lose?

Thus, I did the math
To that critical path….of no return
Because I was not about burning
From the pain of my yearning

We waited no longer
As our lust for one another got stronger
Then we made a command decision
That would require no revision
As we rushed into the house on a mission

Our passion created a fragrance as startling as
A forsaken incision

We devoured each other
Just as though we were only lovers
But we were not
Instead, we were husband and wife
And our passion injected new life
Into our marriage
Our loving always took us away in a carriage

I been solely with her for so many years
And I assume she's been solely with me
Despite her passionate tears

Nevertheless, every time we make love
I think it comes straight from above
Because the newness of each touch
Is as fresh and unique as a dove

So players hear me out
As I begin to make my shout
I get laid all the time

And it feels so new, so pure
So powerfully addictive
But my feelings and passion
Are by no means restrictive

Because I get laid with the same woman
And she gets laid with the same man
Who asked her father for her hand

Every time seems like the first time
And the more we make love
The stronger our lust for one another grows
God only knows
As once again, the next time
Will be just as fresh and pure as…the first time.

This poem was inspired at the passing of my cousin who died unexpectedly at 30 years old while being survived by three children.

<u>The Fragrance Of A Rose</u>

Your life in this world was only for a season
As your time here seemed short but complete
Though some will be quick to explain why
They really don't know the reason
Why the maker you must now meet

Some will talk and many will speculate
About how you conducted your walk
How you chose to regulate

For in the midst of our most terrible pain
We, your loved ones, shall surrender our hurt
And begin to celebrate

You have endured the toughest rain
For the coldest winter did not move your roots
Sudden deaths have a way of leaving
Such a guilty stain
Did we convey to you sufficient love?
Did we ever deny you the truth?

Though we remain disturbed and confused
We will ponder this tragedy for a lifetime
Your sudden death has left no one to accuse
This travesty was a loss

But it hit our family like a crime
Sweetheart, you will be dearly missed
And your legacy of love shall remain

For your young kids will carry the torch
Without a hitch
You have entered into glory
And your flesh transformed to spirit shall reign

Quietly and somewhat peacefully you left us
And why? Nobody really knows
Your life definitely made a tremendous mark
For you were to us like the fragrance of a rose.

Ever met someone on the fly and they left a burning impression upon you? They affected you so much that you wanted to keep in touch but to them you were just a stranger in passing. You come to realize that you may have been a remote stay whereas they were to you a permanent mark.

<u>You Probably Won't Remember</u>

When I walked into the place
I was distracted by your face
As you seemed so seasoned and real

After handling my bizz
I approached you like a quiz
Being shy and nervous, not knowing the deal

I spoke to you in a conservative way
Your attention to me you were not about to pay
Thus I hid behind the memories of my past

You took me back to September
These events you probably won't remember
As Earth, Wind and Fire sang it with a blast

I even met your sista
Then you and I danced to Twista
And we clicked like we were truly meant to be

I was ever so proud
As my heartbeat was so loud

And you and I became sweet serenity

At the club I initially stared
I grabbed your hand to dance
And we became paired
Making me think that for you I cared

I kissed your cheeks
More than just one time
I rubbed your back
Gently touched your behind

You were oh so sweet
So polite and discreet
You are definitely a great gift to mankind

I felt so complete
When I held you in my arms
We quickly became a #1 Best Seller

But I got to keep it real
As you declared you're happily married
There went my thrill
My heart quickly became a cellar dweller

I wanted so badly to swing dance
To the tune of R Kelley
And his Step In The Name Of Love

As your body came between my arms
I felt your breast against my chest
Your hips against my waist
We bonded like a hand united to a glove

I yearned for you
Burned for you
Like a hot fireplace on the coldest day
In the month of December

But don't worry
Don't even be concerned
Don't you dare fret (pause for my teardrop)
Because...you probably… won't… remember.

A male's attraction towards a female. Ladies could this be you? This was one man's attraction to another woman when he stumbled into her on a couple of occasions.

<u>My Pecan Tan (Dime Piece)</u>

She's a perfect pecan tan
Her lips are so thin and narrow
I've got to wear the Red Cross band
I've been wounded by Cupid's arrow

It could be rapid infatuation
Some call it love at first sight
There's been a massive evacuation
She took my heart through the night

When I saw her nice body
My feet were ready to tap
I felt the temptation to be naughty
I tried to lay down my rap

Her teeth were so ivory white
She had the smile of a model
She spurred my sex appetite
My craving advanced to full throttle

She had a very nice height
While packing some perfect weight
Don't let me come off this kite
Deep feelings are what players hate

She's my dime piece, my rhyme piece,
My "Whoa! Check out that behind" piece
My time piece, my crime piece
My sherbet and lime piece

I can't wait to flow her
To grow her, to show her I know her
My muscles will tow her
Stow her and definitely glow her

Is it the stare of her eyes
The thickness of her thighs
Or the bounce of her hips
That gives me numerous butterflies?

Let me restate!
I treasure your height
Oh gurl I'm feeling your weight
I'm trying hard not to fight
At the thought of getting a date

Will you give a brotha a chance
To take you out for a dance
Or will I see you at a glance
And never get to romance

The likes of someone as nice as you
Oh gurl, I'll show you what I can do

So just let me take a ride
I won't impose upon your stride
I'm authentic like leather
Much more valuable than cowhide

So can I get your attention?
And did I forget to even mention
I'll be your solja in retention
I'll let your love serve as prevention

To the foolishness I feel
You see my mind is a convention
I'm letting you know I am for real
So you can clearly see my intention

So as my words come to an end
Can I at least be your friend?
I'm not trying to rip through your skin
I'm just trying to become your next of kin.

This poem makes a political statement for those that are coy enough to receive the message. There is a struggle that exists with African American businesses. We don't do as good a job networking as other cultures do.

<u>Serious Biz</u>

Why is it that we buy from those
Who don't buy from us?
We fuel their cash flows
As though loading up a bus
It's in "them" we truly trust

They strategically plan not to buy from us
They empower their own kind
While we terribly lag behind
Just kicking up a fuss

They know the power of the dollar
Will make us holler
We turn away from our own kind
Won't even support our own collar

In our business world
It seems such a disappointment
How we seem so clueless
We need an injection of business ointment

To make us familiar with our past
And help us remember how we evolved

The other cultures make it last
With economic networks that don't dissolve

Our people don't seem to have the nerve
Time to add business lingo to our verb
Time to teach our own kids
The value of cultural economic networking
This is definitely serious bizz

Its time to understand the game
I'm not falsely misplacing the blame
The true victim is in the mirror
Need I make this point any clearer?

So the moral of this story
In its unadulterated glory
Is that we learn where our dollars are going
For its your mind that the truth will be blowing

As you discover, please recover
From the ignorance of not knowing
Apply a strategy to have dollars flowing
Into a nest where your heritage will be growing

When the political ramifications are exposed
And analytical amplifications are not being told
We must become respondent and informed
We must seek to gain control.

This poem was inspired by the initial reactions to my book cover. I was amazed at how people were so quick to judge while knowing so little about what they were judging.

<u>On Being Judged</u>

When I go to church on Sunday
And I listen to the preacher
I pay my tithes, dry my eyes
I become a brand new creature

True church is so fulfilling
That it sets the soul free
We praise the Lord on one accord
And shout the victory

God is known for being humble
So forgiving and caring of mankind
But church folk can start a rumble
While merely glaring at yo behind

What makes some people so nice and sweet
While in the church pews?
But when they exit those doors of worship
They make drama like the headline news

They judge the way you look
And they stiff you like the plague
But they love yo pocket book
And they sweat you with a craze

Why do they stare at me?
Practically glare at me
Like I don't even know the bible
Then they shoot me with their religious bullets
As though coming straight out a rifle

I may not be where you want me to be
I may not see what you want me to see
But you have no right
According to your biblical creed…to judge me

The moral of this story
Is not to slight true righteous folks
I'm just sick of vain glory
And those hypocritical folks

And if my book causes you to judge me
Simply due to the content and cover
I challenge you with your biased views
To continue to seek and rediscover

That in your narrow minded views
You have created a minority
The very prejudice we seek to overcome
That lies with the traditional majority

I never thought in all my years
Where all my tears were felt
That the bizarre and most prejudice community
Ascended from which I knelt

So let me close as I dispose
Of the intense bitterness proclaimed

Like Alecia said who was not misread
You don't even know my name

By no means am I trying to be roasted up
Nor am I trying to be posted up
But like the Kobe commercial
Understand the reversal

That people will hate you for the same reasons
That people will love you
Thus, your like or dislike is merely your opinion
Get over it!

Have you ever wronged someone, taken advantage of someone, or even neglected someone and you were not aware of the influence of your actions? Your sincere apology can represent true growth on your part.

<u>I Apologize</u>

For the nights that I say I will call you back
But then for some reason I don't

I apologize!
For when I'm supposed to cover your slack
But it seems somehow I won't

I apologize!
For the words that I did not say
But I really meant every one of them
For the stress and the dismay
And the lights I may have dimmed

I apologize!
For the days at the park that we did not spend
All the trouble in the dark that we did not mend

I apologize!
For the times I vowed to come to dinner
But I somehow failed to succeed
I missed your parents, I missed your friends
I messed up indeed

I apologize!
For the life that I live
And the service I don't give
For the actions you easily forgive

I apologize!
For the unreturned phone calls
Sounds of lovemaking beyond hotel walls
For getting mad without a cause

I apologize!
Because I can't seem to meet you half way
I'm in one day and the next I'm about to stray

I apologize!
Please exonerate me from being me
I'm kneeling down on one knee
Your forgiveness means security

I apologize!
For somehow taking you for granted
My devotion to you seemed slanted
And my commitment was often planted
Back in your house where it was stranded
As it seemed like it never accompanied me
But instead it was abandoned by me

I apologize!
For bringing you much hurt and harm
My lack of interest poisoned my charm
My apathy towards you sounded an alarm

I apologize!

For not being there when you needed me
For going everywhere and evading thee
Too selfish to even understand me
Can my confession and apology
Exonerate me?

This poem speaks for itself. It will be an education for some and a mere acknowledgement for others. It's a battle that some have experienced.

<u>Valentine's Day or Doomsday (V-day or D-day)</u>

It's that time of the year
That seems to come around way too fast
When being a player just ain't popular
Because of great demands upon your cash

You can only be in one place
At any given time
On this day, you're in a tedious race
So you must keep a sane mind

You send candy and roses
To all of the above
You send cards and love notes
If nearby, you're tempted to give a gentle hug

You got to make yourself too busy
For any type of appearance
But if you upset that truly special honey
You'll find yourself like a clothing item...
On sale...a clearance

That's right players! It's V-day
But for you, it could be D-day
You are fighting a war

That only you and other players know about

The faithful guys are living stress-free
The dating Vietnam Jungle
They probably know nothing about

On this particular day
So many lies will likely be told
True players may take a fall
For it's on this day that they could be exposed

Just think, she's been bringing all the loving
Some home girls really pay their dues
All to realize, he won't only just clubbing
But he was somewhere secretly rubbing
The feet of women dancing with guilty shoes

True players may have too many women
Well beyond what their pockets can afford
Don't get confused by them wearing white linen
The ice worn around the wrists, ears, and neck
Could possibly be a reward

"You mean I did all of that for him,
And I didn't even get a card or rose?"
No my dear! For his wallet is way too slim
He can't even buy drugs for a congested nose
Not on this day…not during this month

Some may call his ice, gifts
From several sugar mommas
Not baby mommas
Some women truly shower them down

And will even preserve their life
Much like Pocahontas

The women that have the pure juice and ice
They're not eating the international entrée...
White rice

But instead, they are packing and stacking
The very best of foods and material things
They are the ones that's got you thinking
"All he can afford to treat me out to
dinner, is chicken wings?"

Don't get all salty towards me
Don't even bother to take the time and hate
I'm merely sharing for edification
For I don't want this war to escalate

We're fighting in Iraq, very much to our dismay
But once a year, every year
There is a player's D-day
But normal guys call it V- day.

Ladies don't ever take your man for granted. Cherish him as he should be cherished because if you don't, someone else will.

<u>Hoochie's World</u>

Laced down, iced up
Trying to get up in a brotha's cup
Wanna make him give me time
At the end of the night near some streetlight
We're gonna nip and tuck
I'll get my dime

Once I get him all inside
I will invigorate all his pride
There will be no more fronting
No reason to hide
As his cheddar will become mine
While I take him for a ride

Men can be such an easy lay
Whether married or not they love to play
Then they eventually go astray

Ladies if you don't know me
I'll be your worst nightmare
I'm that queen in the streets
That your man provides care

I do the thangz that you don't do anymore
I keep him fascinated and turned on

Because I'm definitely not a bore

So let me tell you what time it is
As I continue to keep the score
I'll be around, I'm not going anywhere
I'm more to him than you were to him before

So keep on stressing on your man
As I help him kick that can
I will make his toes curl
Don't sleep on me
It's a hoochie's world.

I Found A Penny Today

I found a penny today
When I walked to my car
It took my frown away
For a minute I felt like a star

I know the value to some
May not seem like very much
But in the midst of tribulation
I saw in it God's personal touch

For I was at the very pit
Of all my hurt and pain
But this penny was like a rainbow
Flowing down like deliverance on a train

I just needed one chance, one wish, one hug
One dose of power to brighten my path
For I am tired of merely existing
In what feels like a fuzzy aftermath

But through this penny I could see
Just a little bit of hope
It has replaced the bitter urge in me
To just roll over and croak

Though this penny may be just one cent
To me it means so much more
I may not be able to pay all my rent
But it represents to me an open door

Some days can be so dark and dreary
We fail to recognize the need for a hug
It's those times we're most irritable
Those times we're severely critical
Of ourselves and others
We even shun the very ones that we love

But I found a penny today
It served it's purpose in a very humble way

It's not a nickel, not a dime, not a quarter
But I found a penny today
And it brought a rare smile to my face
Now, I'll build on top of that
As I rediscover my way!

No More

I really don't know why
You don't call me anymore
Your loving still has me high
But I been hurt to the very core

I called several times to speak
And all I heard was your recorded voice
My love for you went well beyond deep
I feel you've made another choice

My mind is racked with numerous questions
What did I do to lose you?
I gave you all of my true confessions
There was nothing controversial for review

We last talked on such a positive note
And I was ready to relocate
Then your bags you begin to tote
Your tires found someone else to rotate

It has really blown my mind
I thought we had so much fun together
Being inside you felt like a legal crime
God! It was so good...the best ever!

Now I'm hooked on the feeling
And the emotions of you
My heart was booked for a lifetime
And now I'm feeling so blue

Can you at least give me a call?
Just let me know that you're okay
I'm trying so hard to understand this fall
Why did you have to haul all of you away?

My taste buds no longer have any taste
My desire to date has reached a stand still
But now I feel like shreds of mere waste
Just a burnt piece of meat coming off a hot grill

That's okay! I guess I'll be alright
Hard rejection energizes my drive to soar
I do apologize with all my might
I've got to get over the feeling
That you and I are...no more.

<u>Refuse To Breakup</u>

You think you got all the facts
No need for me to keep talking
I got no time to relax
Because you're planning on walking

Right straight out of my life
As though we had no beginning
I had to let go of the hype
I recognize I'm not winning

You claim I did all the dirt
As though my conscience was numb
I guess I caused all the hurt
You make me feel like a scum

I can't confess that I'm guilty
I did not do what you claim
I know you think I'm so filthy
I can't admit to your blame

But did it ever cross your mind
That you were singing the wrong song
Not trying to come off unkind
But if perhaps you were wrong

I never was a perfect being
All life comes with many flaws
I misinterpreted what I was seeing
When you seemed to show all your draws

I know the evidence against me is strong
But only I know what really occurred
Can you imagine if you are truly wrong?
Can you imagine if you have truly erred?

I'm trying to patch up all of our pain
I want to continue to be your type
I feel the effects of this sinful stain
But when I said "I do," I said it for life

So can we just forgive one another?
Can we bury our troubled past?
Can we let our love be rediscovered?
Can we vow forever to make it last?

So can I share with you a fat and juicy kiss?
Let it confirm our desire to trust and makeup
Because baby, your loving I don't want to miss
And yes! I refuse for us to breakup.

Are You Living A Lie?

I was a product of the hood
Teachers told me I would be no good
Momma did the best she could

James made us bold
As we did what we were told
Black and proud became our mold
Then it became our role

Money was made by the hustle
A dollar in our house made a loud rustle
Religion versus living wrong became our tussle

Controversy was my middle name
I grew up hard and I had no shame
Momma's leash on me would no longer tame

I started running with the big dogs
They seemed to care for me without a cause
That's how I learned to violate the laws

Pretty soon I earned my own cheese
I took out the right hand and arm
To include the sleeve
I also strayed, no longer prayed, on my knees

I somehow made it to the top
My hunger was strong, therefore I couldn't stop
Then after awhile
Greedy ambitions made me drop

Behind the bars with the criminal stars
Was were I landed
The judge was fierce and with the sentence
He pierced, my heart, like it was branded

Back on my knees praying Lord please
Was truly the prisoner's reprieve
Change me now, help me believe

I thought I grew up nice, I wore my ice
Secured my territory so I could earn my slice
Of that proverbial pie
But I clearly lived a lie.

So Into You

You're my sweet chocolate candy
That I crave to taste and bite
Your juices flood my lips like Brandy
Escaping from a lid so tight

You make me feel so complete
When I hold you within my arms
Your nice sexy butt is replete
You have set off all of my alarms

I want to see you real soon
You got my body so addicted
My nature shoots to the moon
All loneliness has been evicted

I cherish that stare in your eyes
They bring me to a quick halt
I miss your deep inner thighs
I'm talking chocolate, strawberry malt

Although I reign from the South
And girl you reign from the North
You got me doing thangs with my mouth
As though I graduated from a course

Can I put in my bid
A resume for an interview?
My love cannot be hid
Sweetheart! I'm so into you.

Prejudice Eyes

I remember when I was little
And my grandmother would tell me
Son, there are lessons you must learn
Listen here and please don't fail me

There are certain people's eyes
That you must learn to avoid
Or they will make you pay drastically
An expense you cannot afford

I must admit initially
I was slow as to what she was saying
Then it hit me like a freight train
That had lost its way while swaying

Don't you dare go across the fence my son
Because love may not be sustained
Society alone will kill your spirit
Society alone will disdain

But one day I saw
With my own eyes so raw
The eyes I could not resist
She was North Carolina fine
My immediate valentine
Unknown feelings quickly would exist

Her eyes were light colored
They practically smothered
The anchored teachings of my very past

I was so drawn to her, so fond of her
Although I kept my distance like I wore a mask

Her hair was long and stringy
Her personality was dingy
Infatuation occupied my soul
We both liked music by Chingy
With her cell she begin to ring me
My feelings clearly got out of control

I found no fault in her
Had no thought in what would occur
But I lusted for the feeling we call love
My eyes could see no harm
There was no urgent alarm
Time had finally come for me to wear a glove

But still I endured
The lessons within became less secured
That was created by my stubborn demise
I eventually learned
That the prejudice I had spurned
Was due to what I saw with my own eyes.

Have you ever met someone where time literally defied the odds? You seemed to have met and had instant chemistry and carried on with one another as though you had known each other for years. You thoroughly enjoyed one another in heart, mind, and soul, although you just met each other. Your actions may have transcended traditional barriers but you both enjoyed the overall outcome.

<u>Some Moment In Time</u>

The sweet taste of her thighs
Kept this brother on the rise
As my heart and my mind
Became attracted beyond disguise

I never felt so drawn, so overwhelmed
So inspired by another who made me so brave
She brought me to another world like heaven
She was mine even after I went to my grave

When we first met in person
We were nothing but strangers
We carried on with one another
Just as though we were together for years
I was like a kid playing with power rangers
Just a cut above shedding little boy tears

Every love song I heard
Reminded me of the time we spent together

Nevertheless, the feeling, the taste
The intimate discourse stayed with me forever

It happened the first day in just a few hours
But don't think less of her nor me
We sparked a uniqueness
That can only be acquired
Like a strange phenomenon
Such as the twin towers

She's on another coast
And I'm here on the East
I'm not known for being a host
But she literally was my feast

I feel for her each day
And I've yet to see her again
But when I read her emails, hear her voice
It's as though she's deep within

Her words of support
Make me nobler than any hero
I'm so tempted to hit the airport
I got to quench this thirst....fa real doe

She don't even have to lobby
For my love and affection
Because loving her is now my hobby
And I know she feels the connection

I crave her like she's a goddess
That does not even exist

Because of her I have become so modest
She's definitely someone I cannot resist

I love her down home expressions
Her tendency to overcome repressions
Though she's going through turmoil
She never succumbs to the depressions

She injects new life into my veins
Brings so much wisdom to my brains
Can you clearly see why
I cannot release the reigns?

On her, if not but only in my mind
I want to be with her, live and grow with her
Have fun with her
Just like that moment in time!

You see some moment in time
We went from strangers to lovers
Our chemistry was ever so strong
And it led us right beneath the covers

She has become my friend
And I adore her very much
We don't talk everyday
But we do kind of keep in touch

No I don't feel bad
For quickly getting so loosely clad
With a stranger turned lover
You see we committed no crime

All we did was reach a plateau
That was for us never attained
Some moment in time.

Have you ever missed someone so badly that when they vacated the primacies, you actually missed them in ways you would not know or understand? It could be from a breakup of a relationship, the loss of a significant other, or the missing of a key family member or friend. The loss in and of itself causes you to be so lonely in ways you could never have imagined.

<u>Not A Day Goes By</u>

That you don't ever cross my mind
I still wish that you were here
I think about you all the time

Not a day goes by
That I resent we had to part
I'm often sad in every way
I still have got you in my heart

Not a day goes by
I keep on looking in the mirror
I don't like what I see
My loneliness for you is clearer

Not a day goes by
I miss that smile up on your face
We used to have all types of fun
You used to make my heart race

Not a day goes by

I think of you like yesterday
That was the time we spent last
That was the time we last played

Not a day goes by
I find this yearning in my soul
I want to be made complete
I need you with me to make me whole

Not a day goes by
Without me wishing and a hoping
I find myself always groping
My mind be working, my eyes be scoping

Not a day goes by
Without me trying to get life back
I'm such a bore to all my friends
I got no juice -- quit drinking JACK

Not a day goes by
I want to replace the gloom inside
I want to dream my life away
I want to be just where you reside

Not a day goes by
If I could just turn back the clock
I would not be so impatient
My heart would not be like a rock

Not a day goes by
It just seems so very depressing
I'm unhappy with so many blessings
I'm always thinking, just always stressing

Not a day goes by
I wish I could take back everything I said
I was so stupid, so ignorant
I must have really lost my head

Not a day goes by
I'm not getting any younger
I'm not eating, not getting fatter
Just a naked spirit crying out
Not a day goes by.

Have you ever fell in love with someone so very fast but in such a natural way? You become dependent upon them emotionally to where they become your primary focus socially and you come to realize that you don't want to live without them. Upon meeting them, they take you to another level of life that you have never experienced before. Then, before long, you realize that you have began to really live life to its very fullest while never experiencing that joy before.

<u>You Begin Me</u>

There is a calmness that I feel
When I look into your eyes
You validate you are for real
My self esteem has taken a rise

You make a man who was seriously hurt
Want to fall in love again
I been out of practice but I'm willing to work
I want to become your lifetime friend

I know you have been turned down
By a couple of men of today
I'm not trying to be a rebound
But my feelings are greater than I can say

I never planned to ever fall in love again
I keep women at a distance
I never allow them to get close within

But instead I've been extremely resistant

But your natural words and expressions
Make me stop at attention
I want to praise you for your impressions
You are worthy of honorable mention

You have the persona of a queen
That demands a double take
And your stare is fiercely mean
You are a deep study….like an earthquake

The juicy thickness of your lips
The succulent roundness of your tips
And the horse powered firmness of your hips
Are alone, a gold mine
This brother will be taking numerous trips
I'll be doing so many flips
To turn back the hands of time

Why? Because you don't complete me
But baby girl you begin me
I'm about to love for the first time
As you receive me
For you are the joy that truly sets a man free

For years I suffered and believed in mediocrity
But your love has produced fantasy on earth
Taking me from a dream to sheer, stark reality

When I'm with you I can't help but to kiss
And rub all over your body
By no means am I trying to be dismissed

By no means am I trying to be naughty

But my mind and my heart yearn to touch you
Like there will be no tomorrow
For you see, I was down and out from my view
But with you I graduated from my sorrow

I want to thank you so very much
For allowing me to touch
And become a part of your life
I hope and pray that someday
You will eventually rise up
And become, without a crutch, my wife.

Have you ever wondered how your end would be? Have you ever dreamed about it? Don't think I'm trying to steer you that way but this poem was an imagination of what the end could be like.

<u>The Aftermath</u>

Sought up, brought up
I thought I would be caught up
To meet him up in the air

I've repented of my sins
Tried to live with most my friends
So truly I should be there?

I kept the faith but not like Job
I studied diligently for my robe
And I tried in life to be fair

Now once I stand in that line
I just pray that this is my time
As I search and peruse everywhere

When I look back on my life
I wasn't that good, I had much strife
But for most people I tried to care

Now I feel like I know the deal
I probably should have been more real
Why did my tongue choose often to swear?

I started to feel like I was alone
I can't reach my friends
Can't use the phone
Though my hand is stretching for a juicy pear

Is this an illusion or is it my conclusion
That I have derived at from being in seclusion?
Why do I seem not to really care?

I'm starting to feel like a spectacle
An old piece of furniture, a collectible
And I feel the looks from so many stares

Dear Lord, is it too late?
I'm in a coffin and they said late great
Before my name
This has got to be some nightmare

Somebody grab me and wake me
Don't let those dark suits take me
I was once so spoiled with such great care

I see my son, I see my daughter
They're both crying like I've been slaughtered
Hey kids why yawl acting so rare?

Oh my goodness! Please forgive me!
I know I'm done but Lord relive me
I forgot to do a will for my kids

I'm so sorry my little ones
I know the state will take my coins
That I truly intended for yawl

Now my heaven will be my hell
As I screwed up and I don't deserve bail
From yawl I don't deserve a call

There's a preacher in a robe who's talking
There are ladies in black hats who are gawking
Can someone help me sit up in a chair?

Tick tock was the sound
Not in my ear but on the mound
Of where my head once used to be

One moment I'm in the garden
The next moment I'm in the church
Can someone solve this mystery?

As I look over the congregation
I'm appalled by the aberration
Of so many who hated my guts

There were many who turned on me
With their tongue and hypocrisy
Which is why I never kissed their butts

Hold up, wait a minute, don't let him speak
He will put a spin on it
He and I never got along

Why in the world in such a small town
And where few are renown
Would they let my enemy up on the throne?

I feel so helpless, so powerless

Because nobody can see nor hear me
But believe me...I'm not lying in that coffin!

But I'm up and about
You can't hear me as I shout
I'm swimming around in midair like a dolphin

Okay enough of you guys' lies
You folks have watered my eyes
With all that fake devotion and commotion

Cause if you really felt that way
I would have known it in my day
When I was alive moving like an ocean

So if you really love someone
And that person is still alive
Don't wait until the funeral
To attempt to revive
All the love you had for them

Convey to folks the love right now
Bury your pride and reflect on how
They are to you such a true and precious gem.

Why Do Women Lie?

She told me she loved me, craved me
Had desires for no one else but me
I was the only game in town

Made me feel so secure
Had me no longer feeling unsure
About myself so I put all my eggs in one basket
Vacating the shelf...bad move
Feeling like a clown

I should have looked harder for the signs
Men are often guilty for these types of crimes
Why was she so bad? Why am I so mad?

I guess those little lies
Became cancer like those Big Mac and fries
She would often tell a guy she would call him
When she had no intention at all

She would often tell vendors
She would buy whatever they were selling
I recognized the little lies
Her perfume I was constantly smelling

I even saw her lie to her girlfriend
About her hairstyle and dress
Then when she and I was alone
All she called her was one big mess

Oh yes, the signs were clearly there, I swear

But I was convinced that with me
She would only share the truth
Boy was I so aloof

How could she lie with so little conviction?
How could she cry with tears of addiction?
To only convey what was not real
Can somebody tell me the deal?

Some men lie but aren't they supposed to?
Just to maintain the player's card?
Just to remain in the crew?

But a woman represents virtue
A woman represents the real
Emotions they can't hide
The other man they won't steal
At least that's the way I was taught to feel
Now I'm so distraught

Can somebody tell me
How and why women lie?
I'm not trying to have a cow
But now that my tears are all dry
I just want to know why?

Guess they have become
What some men have influenced...liars
Just like our own nature

Men stop lying so women can stop crying
So emotions will cease from frying
And our loyalty will cease from dying

We are creating devils in our midst
Can we stop the trend with a beautiful twist?

Women please accept the truth
And don't desire fiction to rule our diction
Let's give an expiration notice to falsehood
It's time for both of us to be real and fairly deal
With our issues that clearly crowd our tissues.

<u>But I Keep On Having These Dreams</u>

Somebody must be praying for me
Slaving up a storm and laying up for me
Because I keep on having these dreams

I'm living a life I never lived
Been drawn into a world where I can't be still
But I keep on having these dreams

My life has turned greater than 360
I'm chasing the sky as I rapidly approach fifty
But I keep on having these dreams

I no longer deal with certain friends of my past
I don't entertain relatives whose love won't last
And I've given up most of my ends

Lack of trust has ruined friendships
Lack of love has destroyed relationships
The future must provide better trends

You see the dreams take me back
To where I once started
The dreams take me back
From whence I have departed
For I have no control over them

The dreams seem more powerful
Than life or death
They make me want to comprehend

What appears to be stealth
I'm not just acting on a whim

Is this the way it feels
When people are praying for you
When they are secretly laying up
And boldly craving for you
While urging you to come back home?

You see my lifestyle has changed
My goals have all been rearranged
I've definitely been going at it all alone

But in my most powerful day
I emerge from my knees because I pray
And nothing seems to stand in my way

My dreams are not quite fair
They are worst when they become nightmares
Which is why I extend the length of my day

Am I a victim of my past
Because my dreams seem to outlast
Current acts of recovery I may have engaged?

The question that arises in all of my surmising
Make me wonder if in me
A war has been waged?

Is this current mode of existence
All about my resistance
To return to the life I once had?

Have I fallen too far from grace?
Am I living a white lie?
Is my current living really all that bad?

At times I feel free to explore and just be me
But life's realities emerge from all seams

I think I live a successful life
Accompanied with a valuable price
But I just keep on having these dreams

In my dreams I'm reunited with my past
But I'm not excited and the joy won't last
Fear catapults to the top

In my dreams I seem more tolerant
I miss my family and friends I now shun
While my pride takes a serious flop

Am I the only one battling this type of struggle?
The dizziness from the nightmares
Have me floating on a stream

Though my life seems more fantasy than real
I'll do my best to stress the authentic appeal
But I keep on having these dreams.

<u>My Name Is Tyrone</u>

I'm the heart throb that makes
A woman's eyes roam
I live in the streets because
I never stay at home
My name....is Tyrone

Ladies always call me on my cellular telephone
Some even holla at me in public
With a secret microphone
You best remember my name
Oh yeah....it's Tyrone

I'm the jodie that your wife
Forever screams about
I'm that baller in her mind
She forever dreams about
I'm the man in her plan
She never leaves home without
You keep on thinking she's out there all alone
My name....is Tyrone

I don't spend any money, my lovers buy for me
I treat em all like my honey and trust me bruh
They all lie for me
I don't have a clone
My name….is Tyrone

While you watching all the sports
And attending all the games
I'm knee deep up in her shorts

Like my blood is flowing through her veins
I'm as firm as a precious stone
My name….is Tyrone

So just keep on ignoring me
And looking over my name
Keep on underestimating and calling me lame
This tiger cannot be tamed
I'm the one that's singing your girl a nice song
My name....is Tyrone

Keep thinking I'm just a blue collar worker
With absolutely nothing going on
I'll pretend as though you're right
You no longer need my insight
Just remember
My name….is Tyrone

I'm her massage therapist, her beautician
Her counselor, her preacher and her teacher
I play all roles for her, keep her warm like a fur
Keep on acting like you all up on the throne
My name….is Tyrone

You keep on working all the time
With your vision all blind
I'll do all the crimes for her just like Al Capone
But just remember
My name....is Tyrone.

Why Am I So Sad?

When joy succumbs to sorrow
Eyes seem to borrow water from the sky
To produce tears
Why am I so sad?

Still alive but my health is not great
Nevertheless I've learned to appreciate
The small factors, not reactors
That extend my years

Sometimes I suffer from depression
Being recluse with life's economy in recession
Trying not to become prey to my regression
Why am I so sad?

I sometimes don't want to participate
In life's activities but instead just evaporate
So I won't have to fabricate the truth
Why am I so sad?

My mind takes me back to my childhood days
When life was such fun without all the haze
The blues were the theme for existing time
Such simple songs with such simple rhyme
Why am I so sad?

I once buried myself in the walls of the church
I let religion form me and protect me from hurt
Was life really that simple?
Irritation was like a pimple

But I was happy, not sad…
Why am I so sad?

My spirit is ever yearning
My flesh feels like its burning
My body and mind are forever turning
And tossing in bed
Hear what I said?
I don't sleep at night
But instead I think aloud with fright
Why am I so sad?

I once liked normal things
Like women, cars, and fancy things
But now they all bore me
I no longer drink a Forty
Much less I lost the taste for alcohol
And I don't recall my last urge
Why am I so sad?

Gas prices are way too high
The people that I meet can be so dry
I sometimes don't even want to try
My mind is working 24/7, I dare not lie
Why am I so sad?

Material things no longer move me
The bounce of her butt no longer grooves me
The ounce of my gut
Soothes me but it shouldn't

I find myself in a state of nonexistence
Where I am often quietly in resistance

To everything and everyone
Why am I so sad?

Friends come and go just like a hoe
Almost like the hunting season for a doe
But nobody makes me interested
But instead disinterested
Why am I so sad?

So may I cling my focus to a positive thing
One step at a time, just let freedom ring
As I sharpen that tool for which brings me joy
As I denounce being a fool
And engage in the ploy
Of making myself glad, not sad

God, I know you have a great part
In my brand new start
As I learn to impart your word in my heart
And renew a spirit that somehow
Became worn and torn
By the hustle of life, a misguided wife
And undetected strife

I long to change my words from
Why am I so sad, to why am I so glad
With a smile on my face
A deep expression of grace
God's place in my heart so my joy can embark
Upon new life
Is it possible that the key to the question I ask
Is purely based on such a spiritual fight?
Why am I so sad?

<u>Left The Strong</u>

Somebody say it's not true
My mind is trying to decide
Why haven't I heard from you
My feelings are about to collide

I keep calling your phone
I keep getting your voice mail
I wonder what's going on
You got me not feeling well

I thought I took care of you
In such a very special way
What's up with this pick-a-boo?
I thought the games went away

Now what am I supposed to think
I'm starting to feel rather used
I closed my eyes just to blink
But then I missed all the clues

I guess I'll ease on down the road
I guess you got what you wanted
Thought I chose a prince not a toad
I felt so stupid how I flaunted

How good a man you were to me
I missed the mark on this call
I no longer have victory
My joy somehow hit a wall

I can't even ignore your words
You said I was fire department fine
Because when you looked at me
You burned for my nice behind

Now I'm fishing like the birds
Just hovering over the ocean
My lips are dry without words
Although I used plenty of lotion

So Tyrone, be gone
And I hope you get along
With those weak minded sistas
Because you definitely left the strong.

**Oh No She Didn't
(Reply To Poem Above)**

Oh no don't get it twisted
Because you're about to be listed
In the real estate pages
Because I'm just about to dis ya

I'm talking foreclosure baby
Because ya ain't in the Navy
And ya need to stop acting
Like ya had lots of gravy

Because it is what it is
And my biz is my biz
And you not Michael Jackson
And ya show ain't the whiz

No I didn't leave the strong
All I left was the stingy
Because you're cheap and so wrong
And ya mind is so demented

I just asked you for a bill
Just to help me pay my note
My drive you quickly killed
So my bags I had to tote

Like I was all about the ends
Because I'm not about the skins
So you gonna front on a brotha?
Didn't even let me make amends

So take yo government check
You ain't nothing but a wreck
Next time ya holla my way
Ya betta come with much respect

So with ya next male victim
Don't you try to be so fly
Because if you rolling big bills
You don't got to scream high
Just do the darn thang
And you might reach the sky

So just let me close
With my nose all froze
From the anger of your words
And yo cheap panty hose

You need to stop playing rich
Because you ain't nothing but a snitch
Walking round all pretentious
And you walk with a twitch

As I said once before
As I even out the score
Let me emphasize to you "no more"
As I walk out that door

You made me burnt and crispy
And no I'm not at all tipsy
Got my mind all vindictive
From ya lust and sedition

Please lose my number
And try to remember
That I'm not like yo average dude
That can be so rude
I'm more special and rare
Like the month of December.

The Man Barack Obama

The political canvas in America is
changing, I hear and I've been
listening
There are several sharing opinions,
their words in the air have been
glistening

Will Hillary be the first female
president as history is about
to be made?
Could Barack be the first black
president? Has our country evolved
to this age?

Hillary has walked those White
House halls, her Senate record looks
very good
Is Obama ready for the challenge? His
grassroots stem from Congress to
the hood

And of course Hillary has her
husband Bill while Obama has his
wife Michelle
There may be good qualities in both
of them, take note as inquiring minds
swell

Something miraculous is truly
happening, a lot of folks will
definitely live to see
The mindset of our people has
changed, that's the way it's going
down in history

Young people are actively
involved, first time voters have
literally swamped the polls
We won't settle for the same old
rhetoric, not holding politicians
accountable has taken its toll

Our people are engaged in
conversations, and will tell you why
they are Republican
or Democrat
The economic crisis has awakened
the sleeping giant, and there will
definitely be no turning back

Though Senator MCcain will wage a
tenacious fight, for his military
record is sound and replete
Obama has the goods to show us all a
better light as the party calls for
Hillary to retreat

Even though Hillary is both elegant
and tough and she appears to be a

wonderful momma
Our nation is ready for overall

change, neither two can touch
the man Barack Obama.

Jerome Redd

More Works Of

Bathwater Press Publishing, Co.

Join our team at www.g-natti.com

We are making dreams come true while publishing books of all genres.

THE
CARTERCHRONIC
Til Death Do Us..

GALUMINATTI

Broken Ankles
Where The Court Is Therapy

A
Kid's
Novel
BY
FENNELL

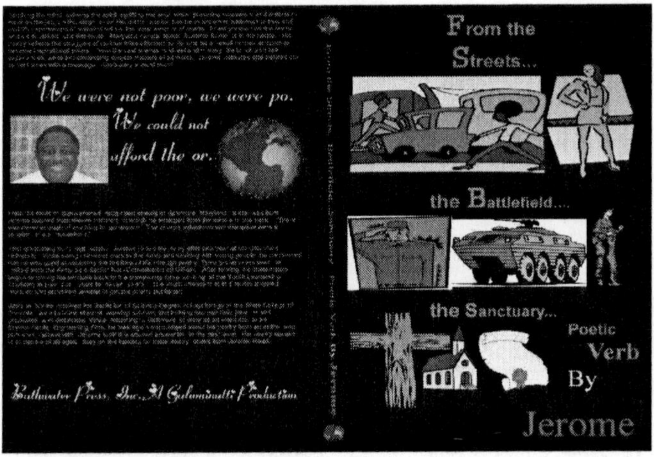
We were not poor, we were po.
We could not
afford the or.
Bathwater Press, Inc., A Galuminatti Production
From the
Streets...
the Battlefield....
the Sanctuary...
Poetic
Verb
By
Jerome

You Begin
Me
GALUMINATTI

Salty Roots...
Seeds of Darkness Erupt
By
Galuminatti